Our Earth Has a Voice

Our Earth Has a Voice

Written and Illustrated by Kime

The contents of this work, including, but not limited to, the accuracy of events, people, and places depicted; opinions expressed; permission to use previously published materials included; and any advice given or actions advocated are solely the responsibility of the author, who assumes all liability for said work and indemnifies the publisher against any claims stemming from publication of the work.

All Rights Reserved
Copyright © 2016 by Kime

No part of this book may be reproduced or transmitted, downloaded, distributed, reverse engineered, or stored in or introduced into any information storage and retrieval system, in any form or by any means, including photocopying and recording, whether electronic or mechanical, now known or hereinafter invented without permission in writing from the publisher.

Dorrance Publishing Co
585 Alpha Drive
Pittsburgh, PA 15238
Visit our website at *www.dorrancebookstore.com*

ISBN: 978-1-4809-3386-6
eISBN: 978-1-4809-3363-7

"This is my Father's world,
and to my listening ears,
all nature sings and around me rings
the music of the spheres."
Maltbie Davenport Babcock, author
(Written before his death in 1901).

Our Earth Has a Voice

Jump off the couch,

turn off the TV;

nature is telling a tale of footprints

left in warm summer's dust,

crisscrossed by ants running free.

A tale of someone

who sits in a barn full of hay,

playing their flute on a sun-filled day.

The Earth has a voice;

its name is "Nature".

It speaks to you and to me

of walks at dusk

where hushed shadows grow;

hear the plunk of raindrops on leaves.

In the tinkling of water

over bright pebbles below,

where mermaids and wishes

and bright pennies go.

Earth has a voice;

its name is Nature.

It's calling to you and to me

in a meadow of flowers,

shouting their colors.

In the fairy-fire's glow,

from the moonlight on snow,

in the crack of cold in the trees.

Down moss-covered steps,

by the croak of a frog,

dance to the song on the breeze.

Love the Earth for it is alive!

Earth has a voice in nature; you'll see stores of adventure for you and for me.

Draw a Tree

Draw a Flower

Draw a Bird

CPSIA information can be obtained
at www.ICGtesting.com
Printed in the USA
LVHW070243010519
616207LV00019B/250/P